The Penguin

Summer is nearly over in Antarctica.
Out in the sea, large groups of emperor penguins
are hunting for fish, krill and squid.
Nero is one of many thousands of penguins
who live on the ice-covered edge of Antarctica.
For many weeks, he has been eating all he can.
Winter is coming, and then he will not eat at all.
Sometimes Nero dives to the sea-bed far below,
in search of a large, juicy squid.
Sometimes he hunts shoals of fish with his friends.
His streamlined body moves swiftly in the water.

Suddenly, a leopard seal bobs up among the penguins.
Emperor penguins are his favourite food.
Nero swims off as fast as he can go,
paddling with his flipper-like wings.
Penguins can swim at 50 kilometres an hour,
but they cannot fly at all.
Just in time, Nero reaches some ice.
He leaps up, flapping his little wings.
He hooks his sharp beak into the ice,
and pulls his heavy body up the slope.
He has been lucky to escape
from those snapping jaws,
and wicked, pointed teeth.

When the antarctic days get shorter
the penguins gather on the ice.
They turn their backs to the sea
which is their only source of food,
and move off slowly inland.
They waddle on their short legs,
and slide down icy slopes,
marching to the breeding grounds.

The journey to the breeding grounds takes many days.
Thousands of penguins go there every autumn.
First the males arrive, followed by the females.
Nero and other male emperor penguins
court females until they all have partners.
Nero bows his head, and flaps his wings to his mate.

A few weeks later, Nero's mate lays a large white egg.
The male penguin has the task of hatching the egg.
His mate passes her egg to Nero.
She rolls it off her feet
and Nero takes it quickly.
He tucks it under a loose fold of skin, or pouch.

The female penguins go back to the sea to feed,
leaving the males to hatch out the eggs.
For sixty days, until the chicks hatch out,
the male penguins carry the eggs on their feet,
tucked snugly in the pouch.

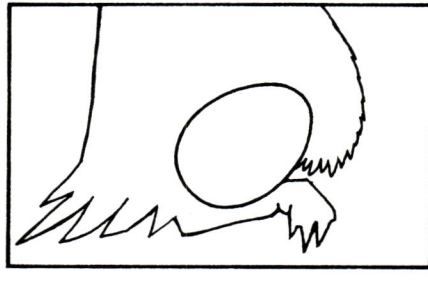

Nero must learn to walk with the egg.
He must not trip or fall
or the egg will crack on the ice.
He shuffles around as well as he can.

Now the terrible antarctic winter has arrived.
Every day there are icy winds and snow.
With their backs to the wind, the penguins
crowd together to keep warm. Those on the outside
shuffle towards the centre; when they are warm
they move back out to the edge.

At last the penguin chicks hatch out.
They are covered in fluffy grey down.
Nero keeps his young chick warm
beneath his loose fold of skin.
Nero has not eaten since he left the sea,
more than three months ago. But he makes
some milky food in his crop to feed the chick.

Then the mother penguins return from the sea
to take over the feeding and care of the chicks.
They have brought more food in their crops.
Now it is Nero's turn to go back to the sea.
He and the other male penguins are very tired.
They have lost most of their fat during the winter.
They plod on wearily towards the sea.
Soon they will feed once more.

Every day, the chicks grow stronger.
As soon as their feathers are thick
they leave the shelter of their mothers
and huddle together in large groups.
Nero and his mate take turns
to go to the sea for food.

When the chicks are four months old,
their feathers are thick and waterproof.
The chicks and penguins move slowly
towards the sea.
They are ready to play and hunt
in the cold antarctic water.

Some facts about penguins

Emperors are the largest of the penguins.
They live in the cold of Antarctica.
All penguins live south of the equator,
in cold seas which contain plenty of food,
such as shrimp-like creatures called krill.
The only penguins north of the equator
are in zoos and in wildlife parks.
Some, such as the Adelie penguin,
build rough nests to hold their eggs.
King penguins, like emperors, carry eggs
around with them on their webbed feet.

Nero is a large bird, over one metre tall.
In summer he weighs over thirty kilograms.
In winter he goes for months without food.
He lives off the layers of fat on his body.
His scale-like feathers keep him warm.
They are both waterproof and windproof.
Each summer when he moults, Nero must stay
on land until his new feathers have grown.
In the icy sea, he would die of cold.
Emperor penguins hatch their chicks
away from the sea, during the dark winter.
They are safe there from enemies
because few other creatures could survive.

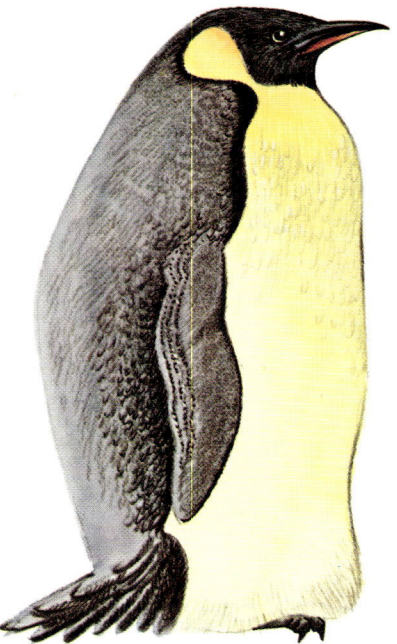

Emperor penguin

Rockhopper penguin   Adelie penguin   Chinstrap penguin   King penguin